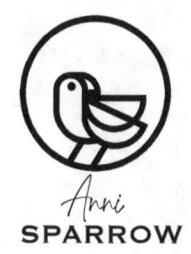

Anni
SPARROW

Dot to Dot
experience

JOURNEY THROUGH
EUROPE

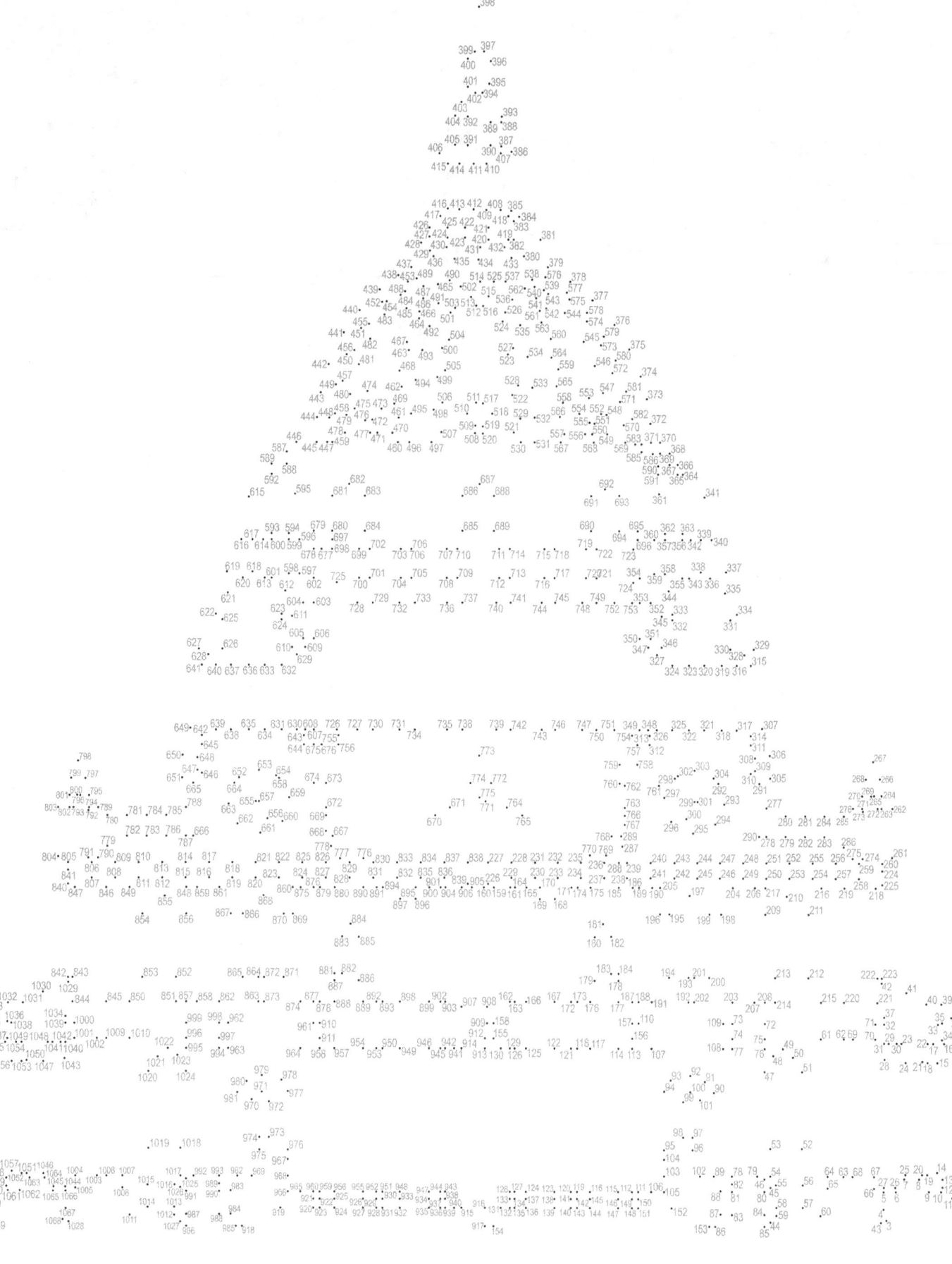

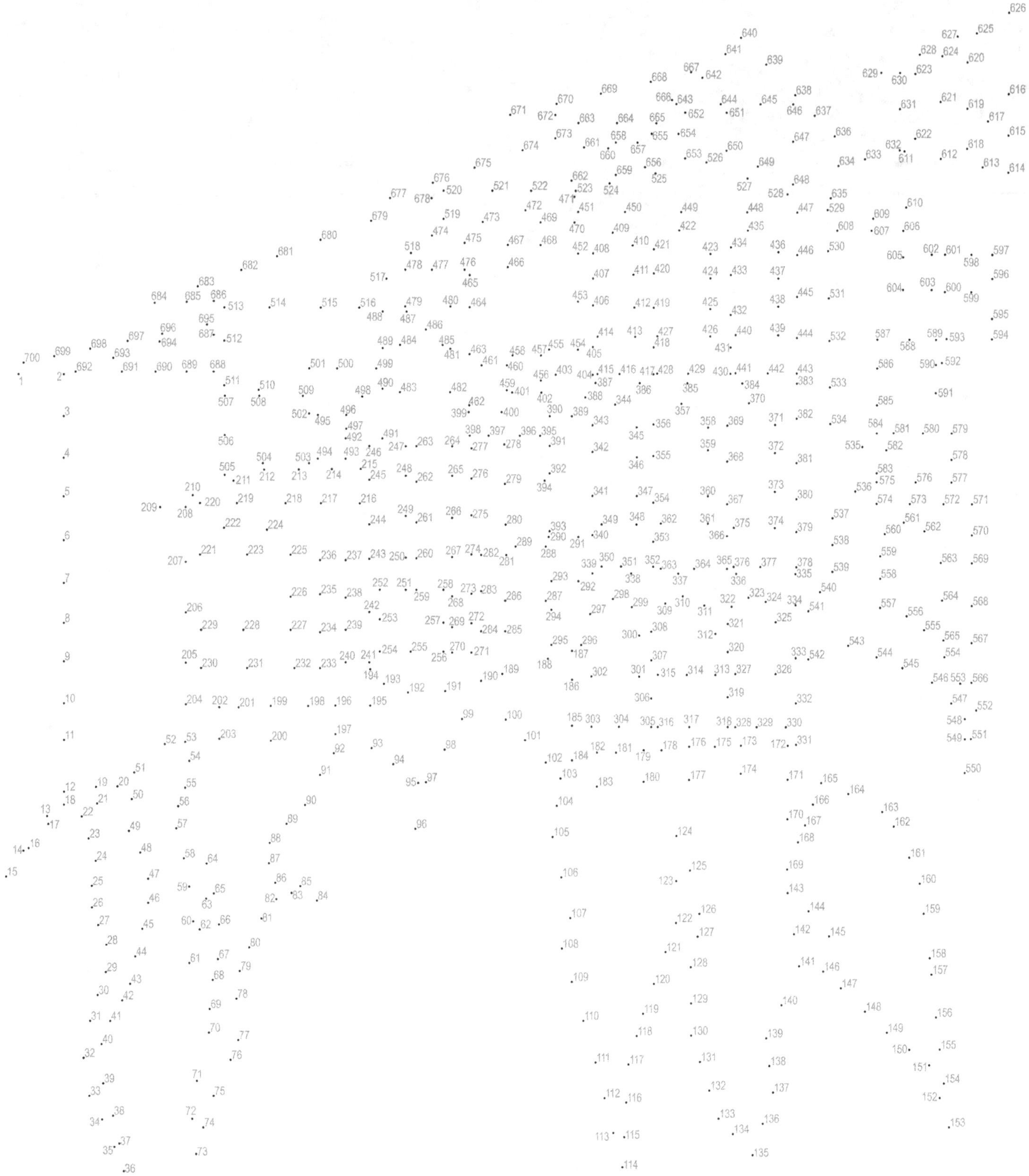

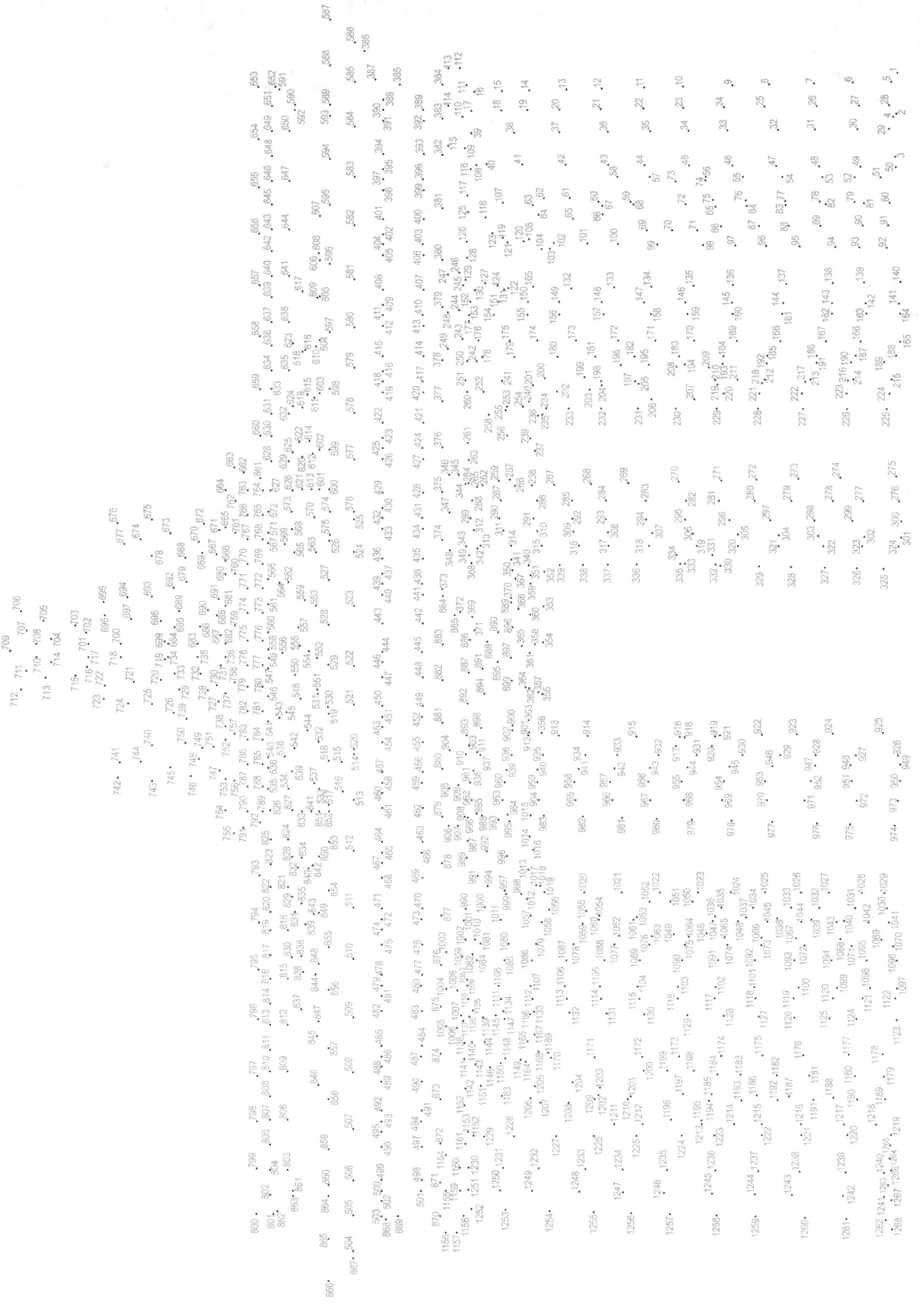

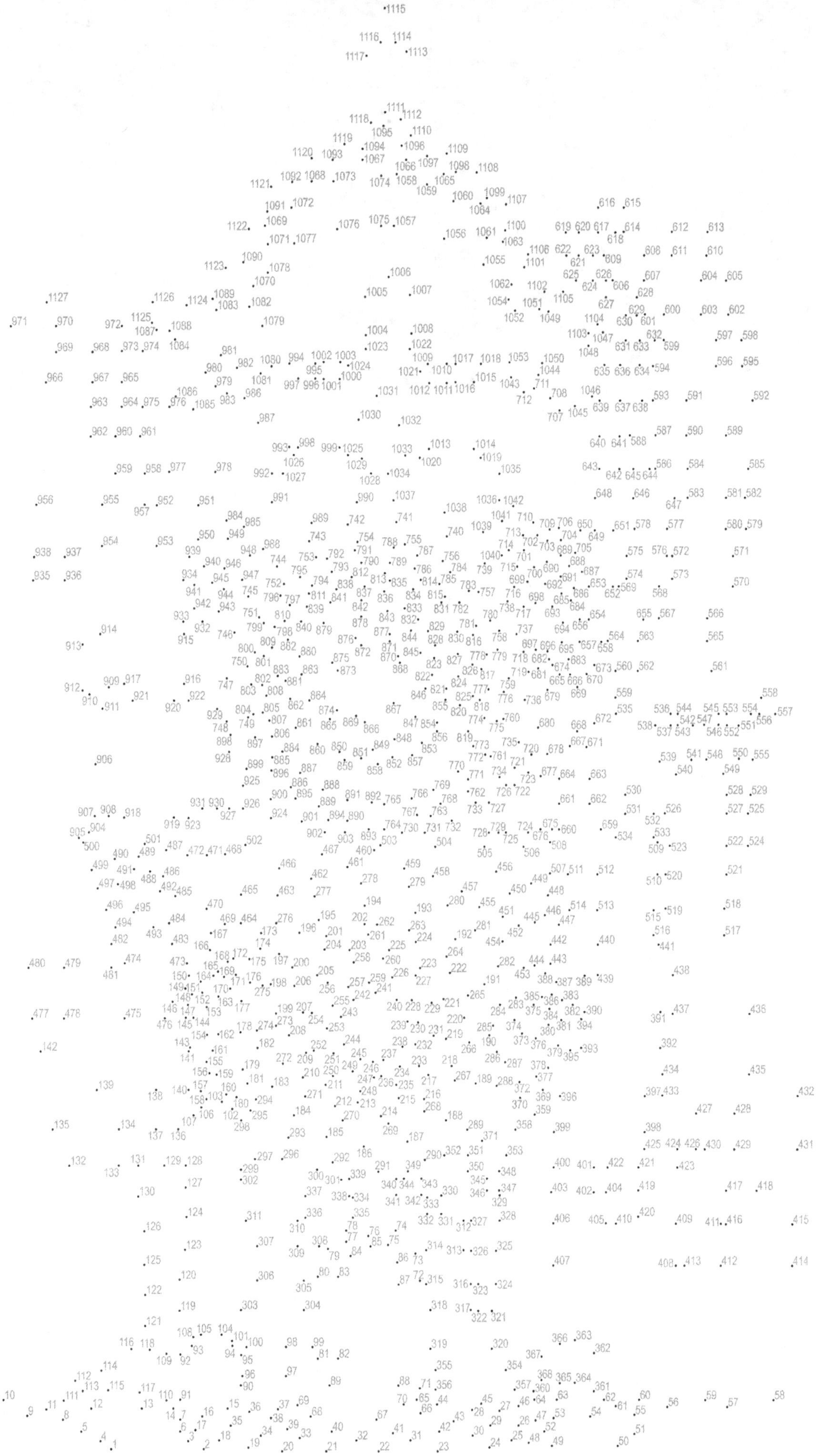

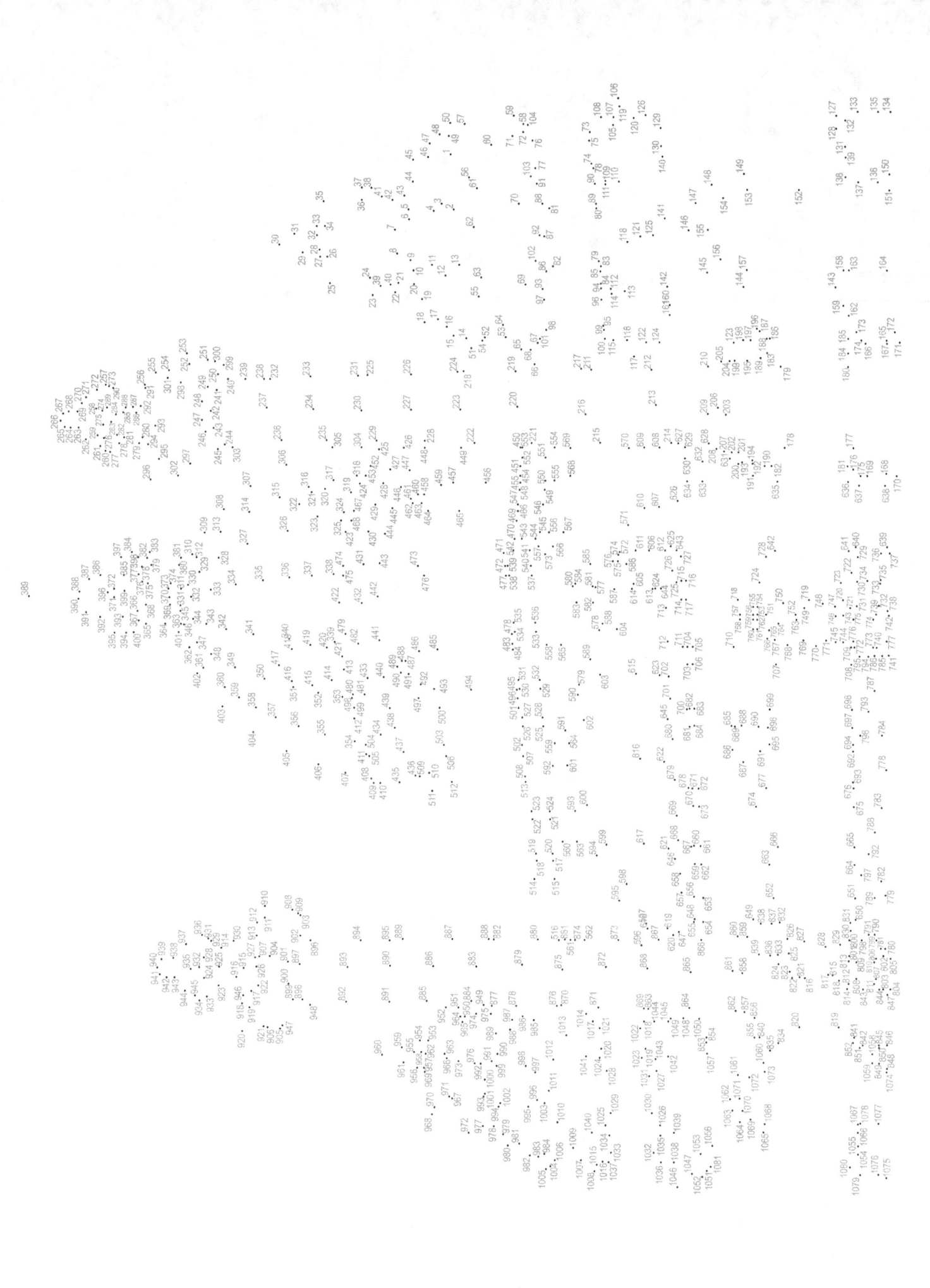

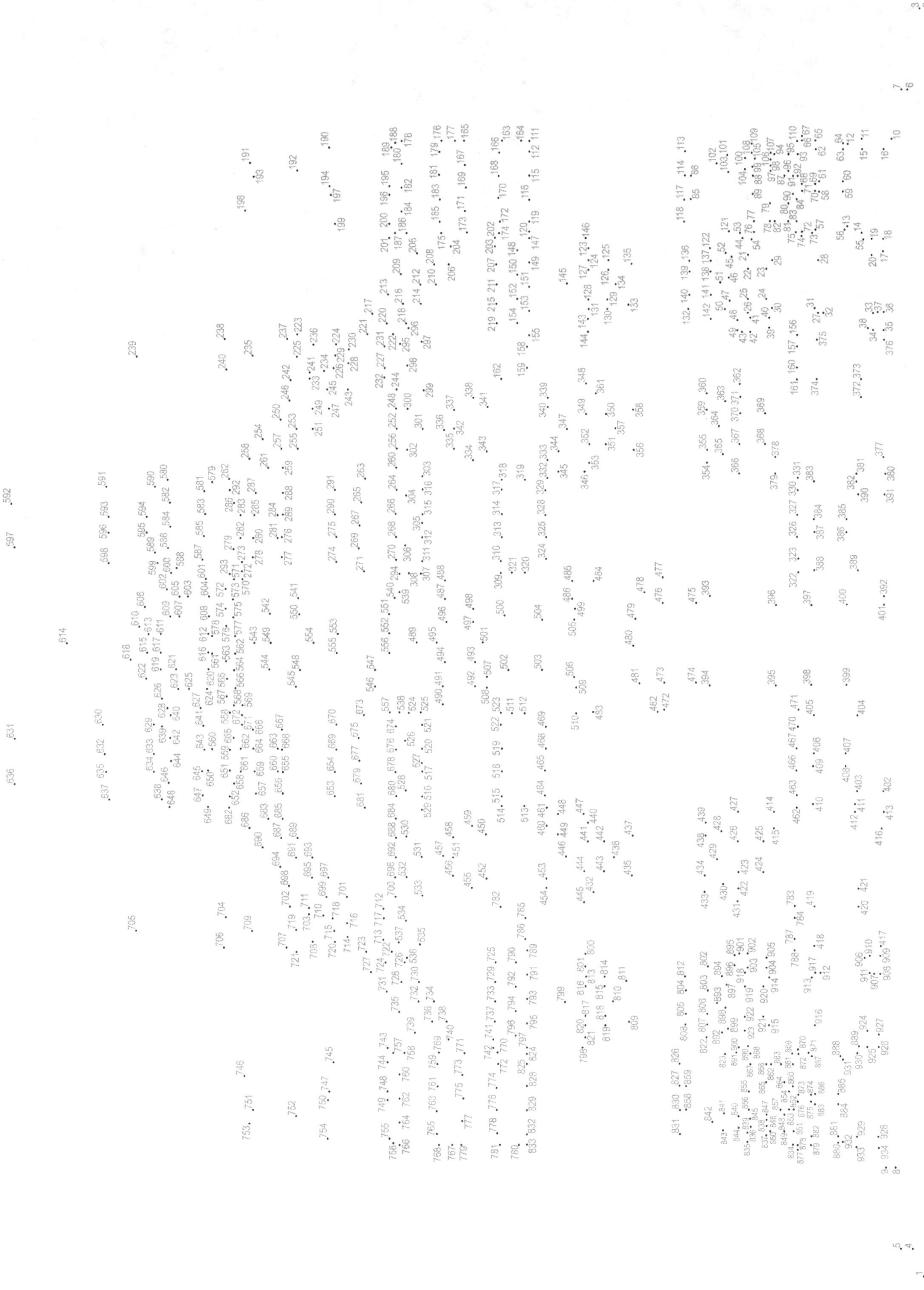

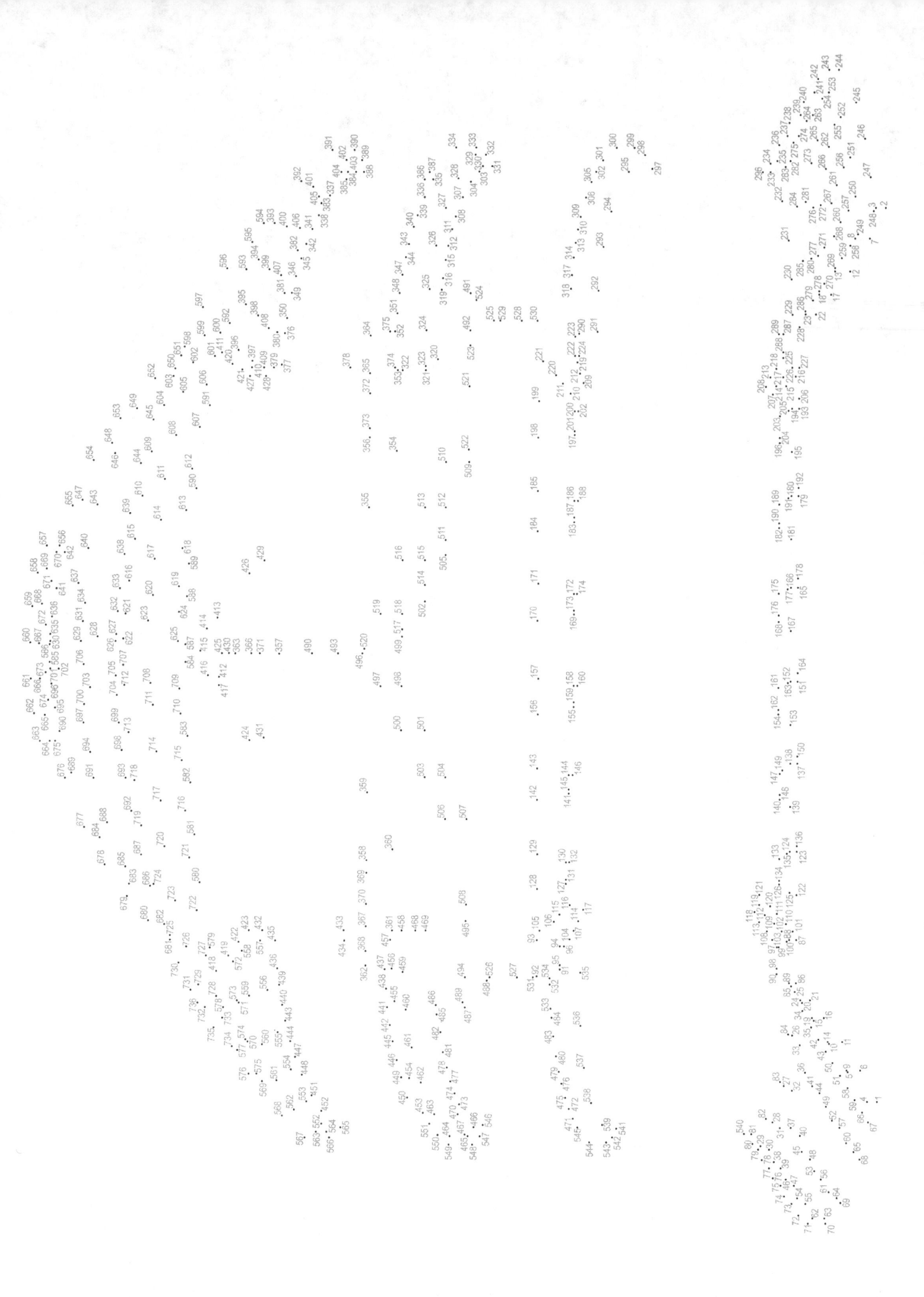

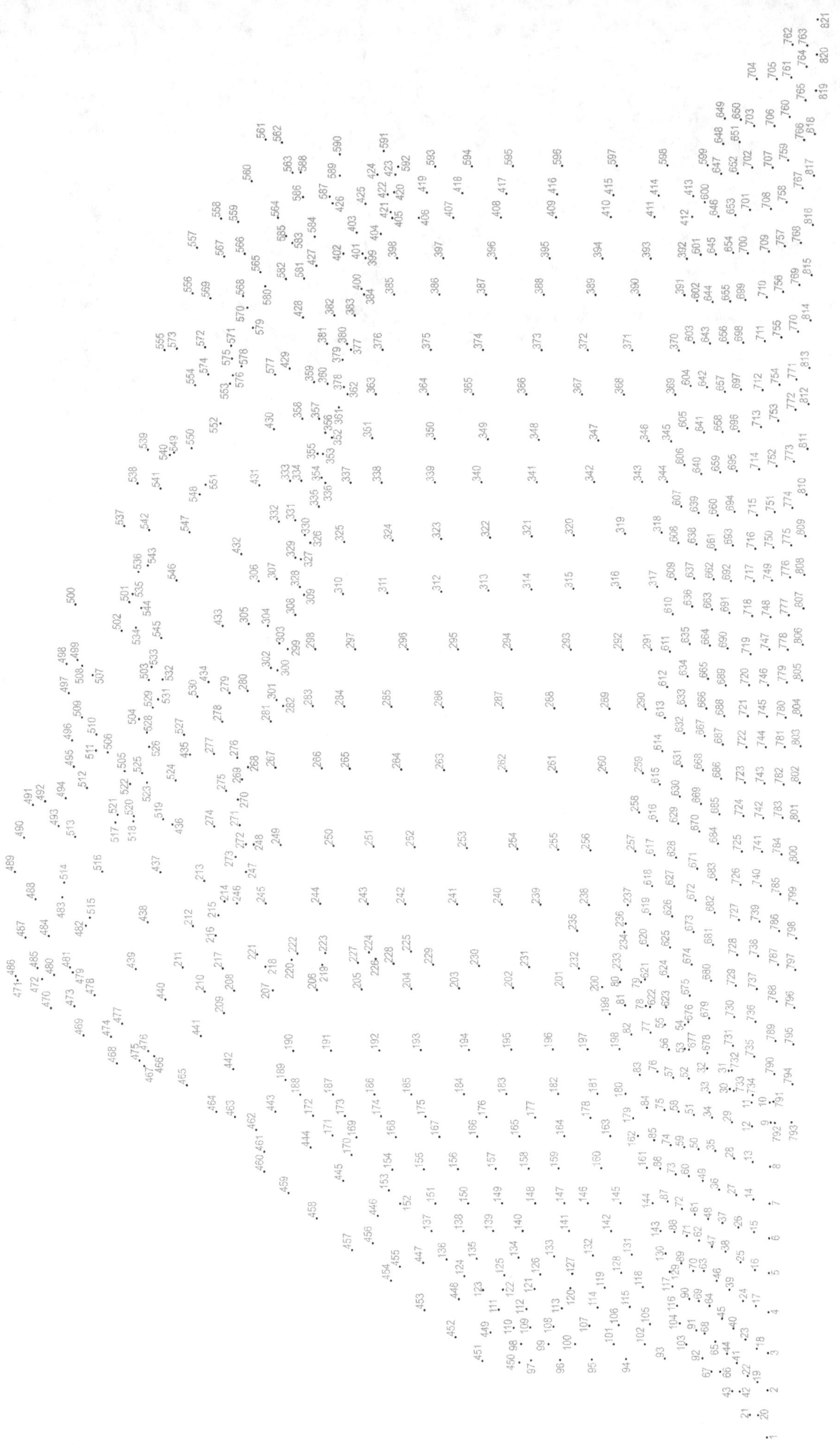

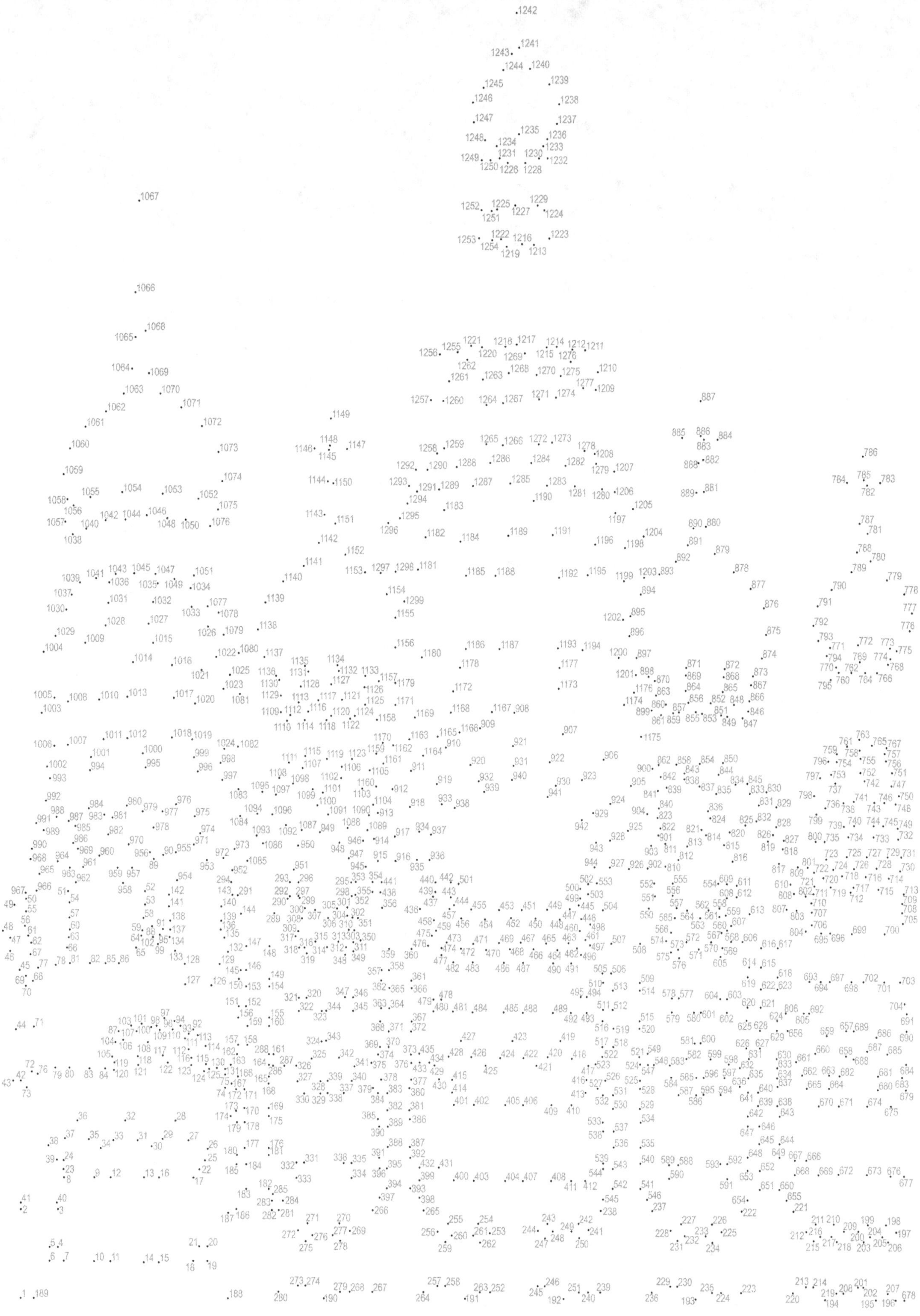

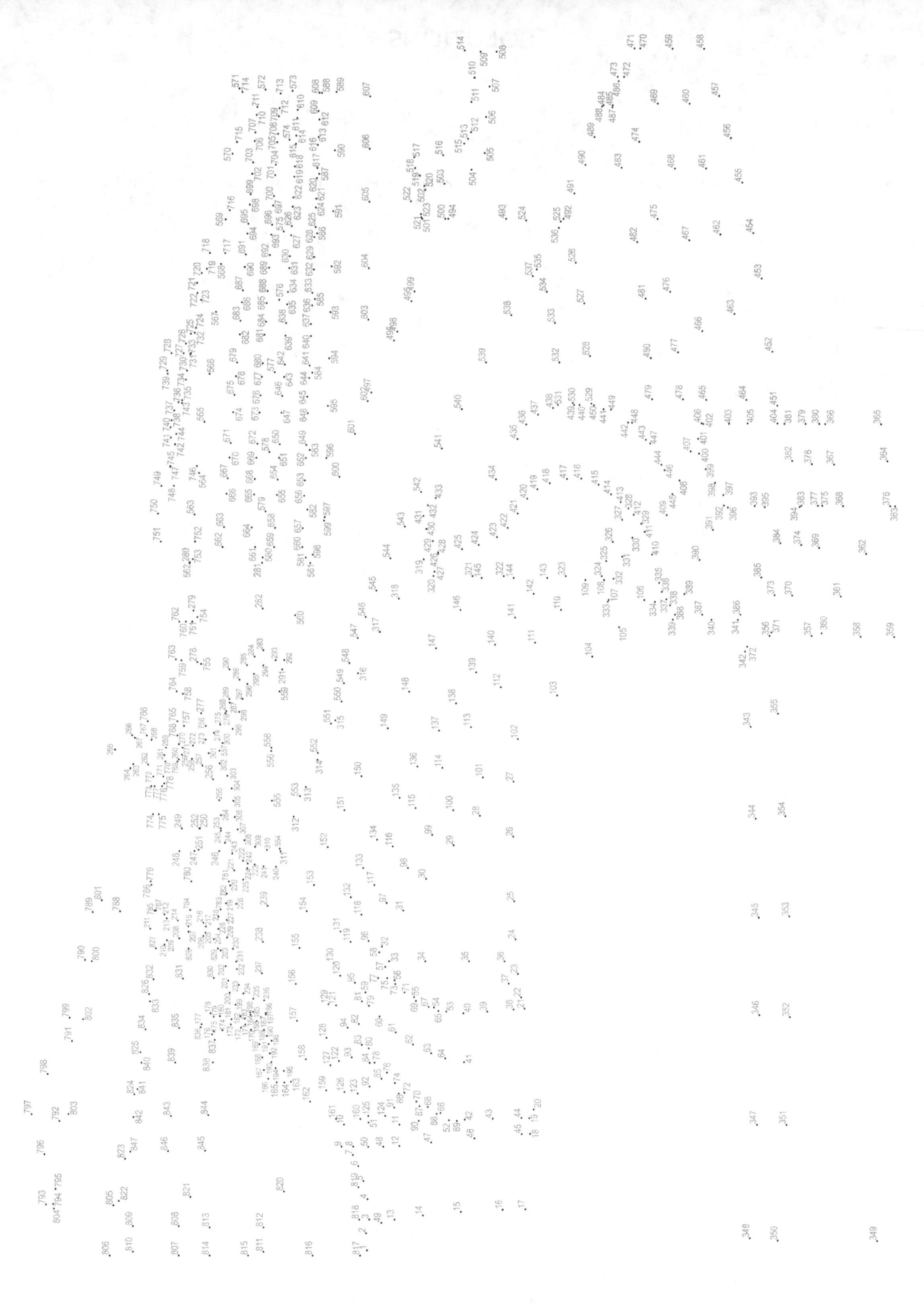

SOLUTIONS

Page 3: Tower Bridge, London, United Kingdom

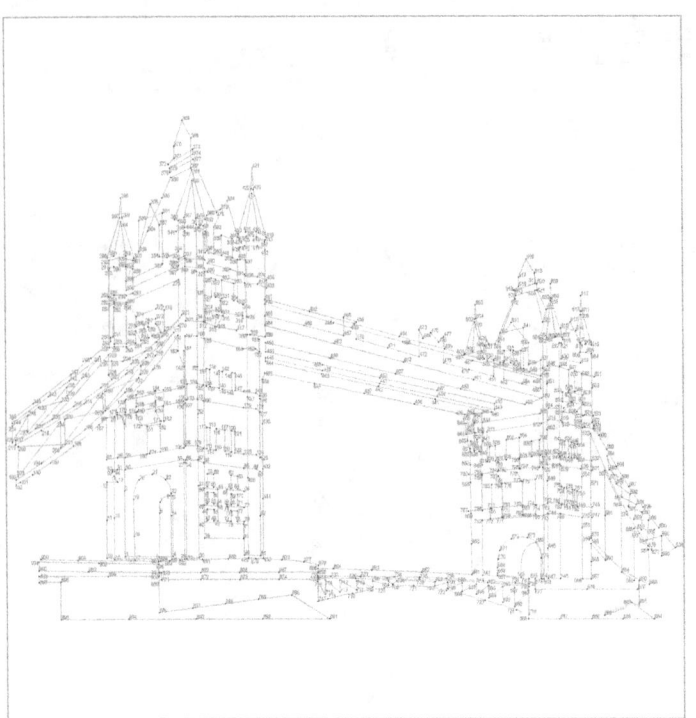

Page 5: St. Paul's Cathedral, London, United Kingdom

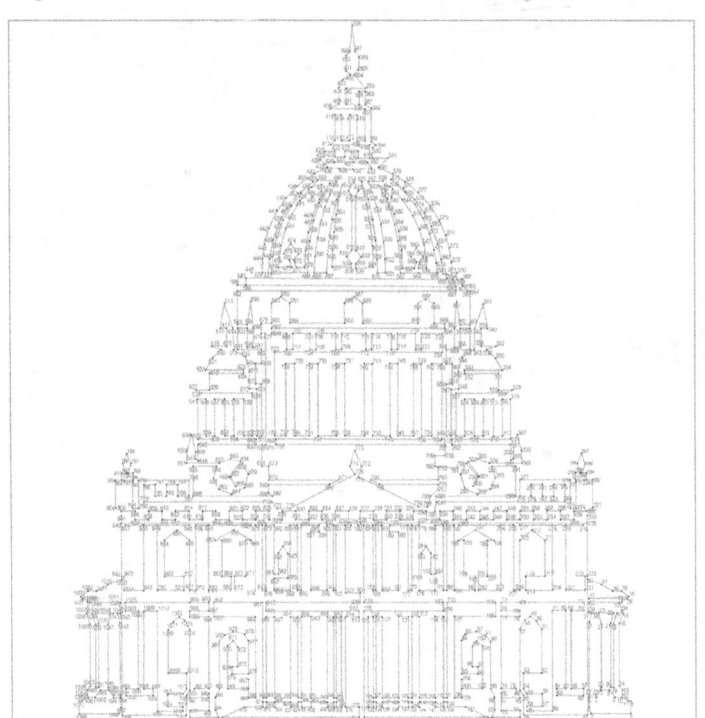

Page 7: The London Eye, London, United Kingdom

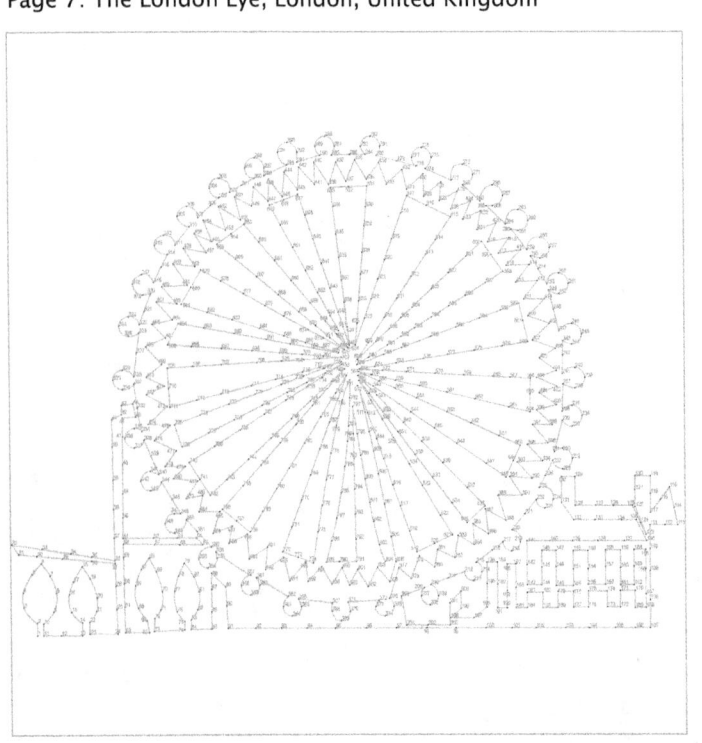

Page 9: Cuenca, Spain

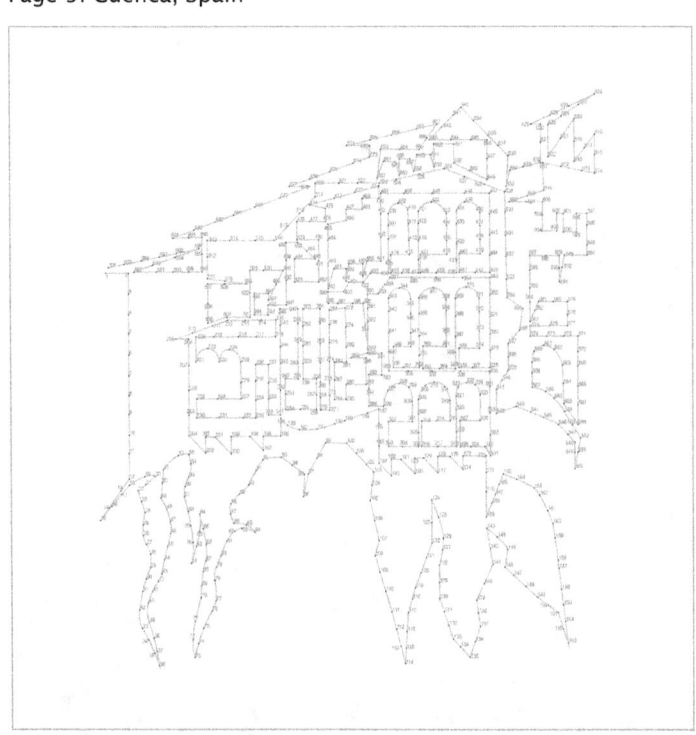

SOLUTIONS

Page 11: Casa Mila, Barcelona, Spain

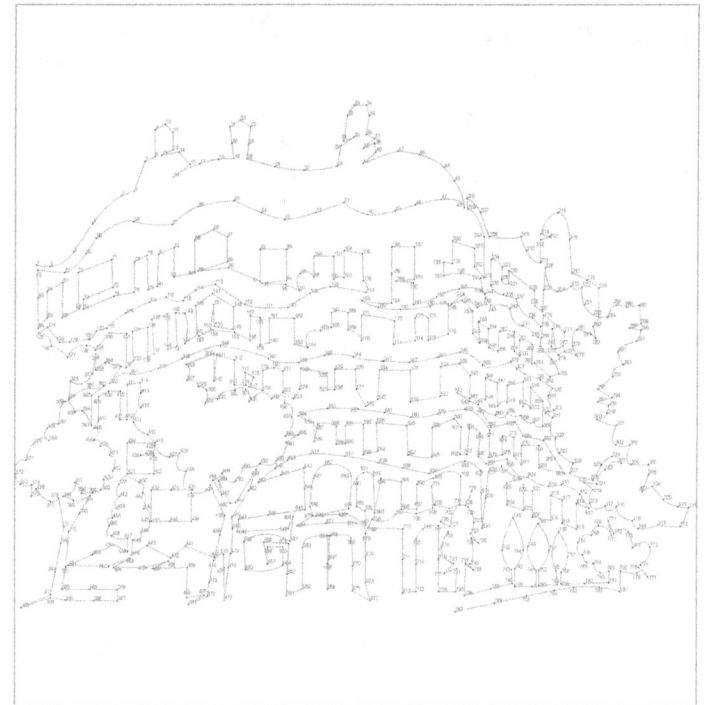

Page 13: Cologne Cathedral, Cologne, Germany

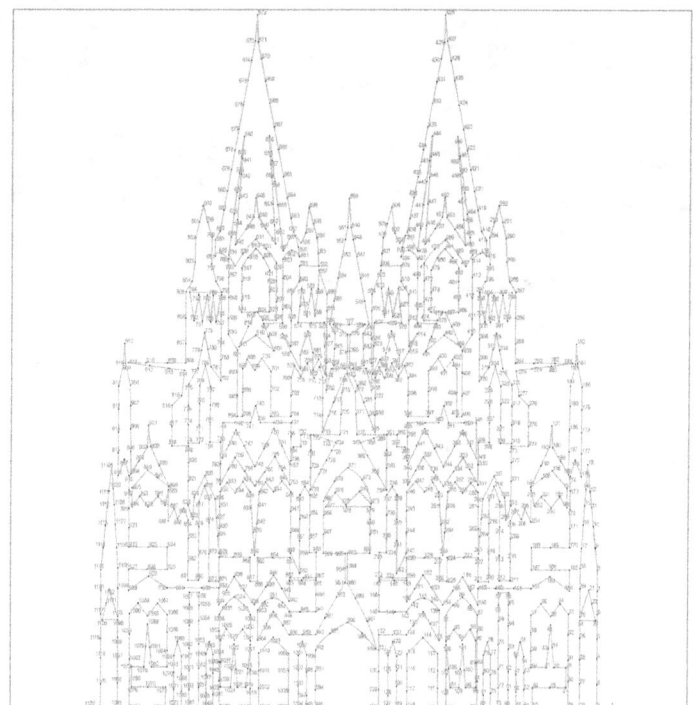

Page 15: Berliner Fernsehturm, Berlin, Germany

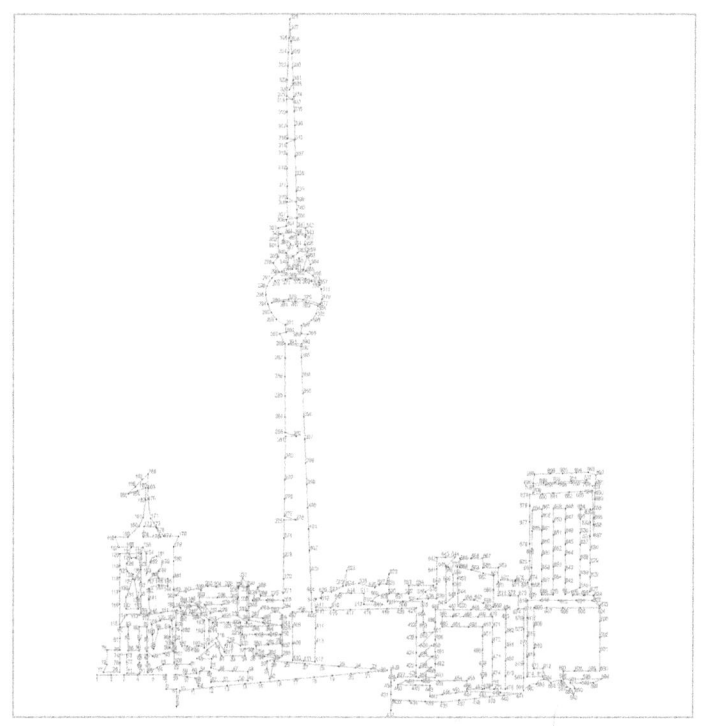

Page 17: Brandenburger Tor, Berlin, Germany

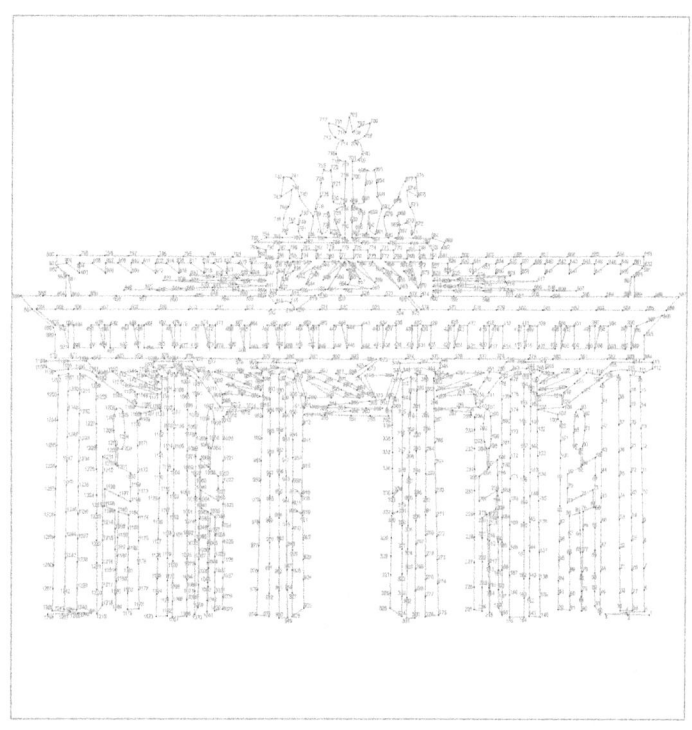

SOLUTIONS

Page 19: Prague Astronomical Clock, Prague, Czech Republic

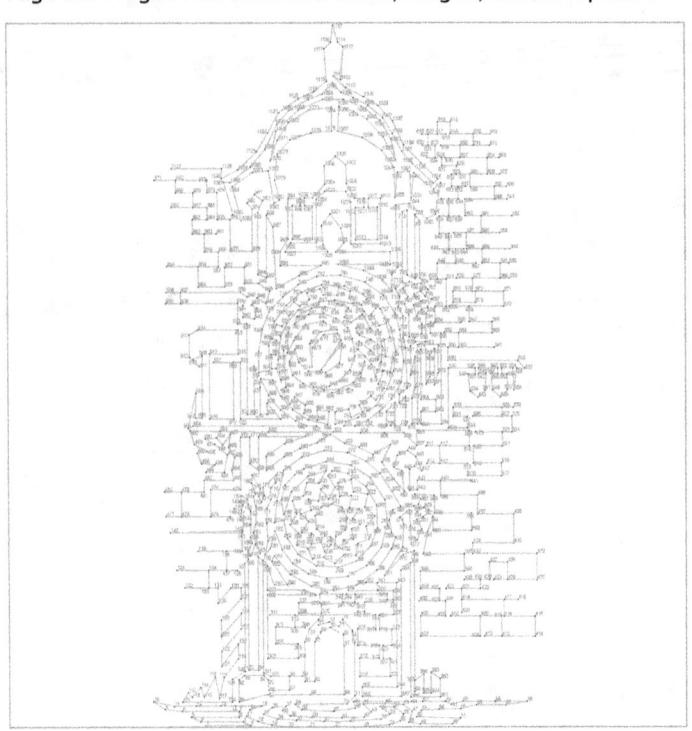

Page 21: Hundertwasser House, Vienna, Austria

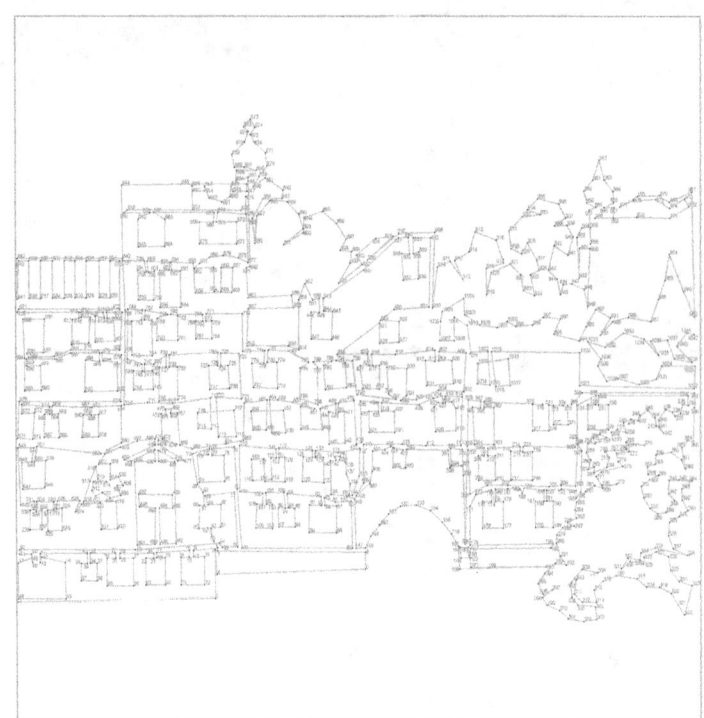

Page 23: Karlskirche, Vienna, Austria

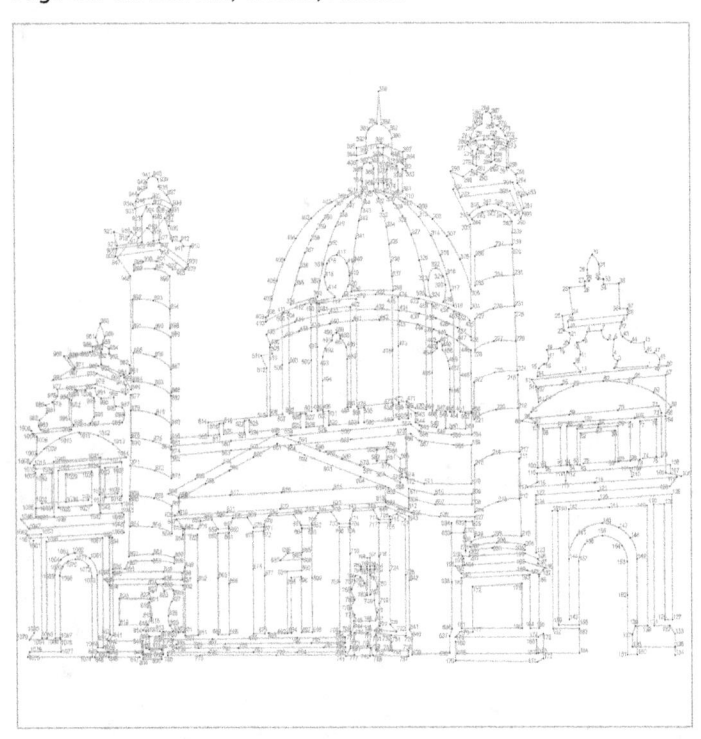

Page 25: Parliament Building, Budapest, Hungary

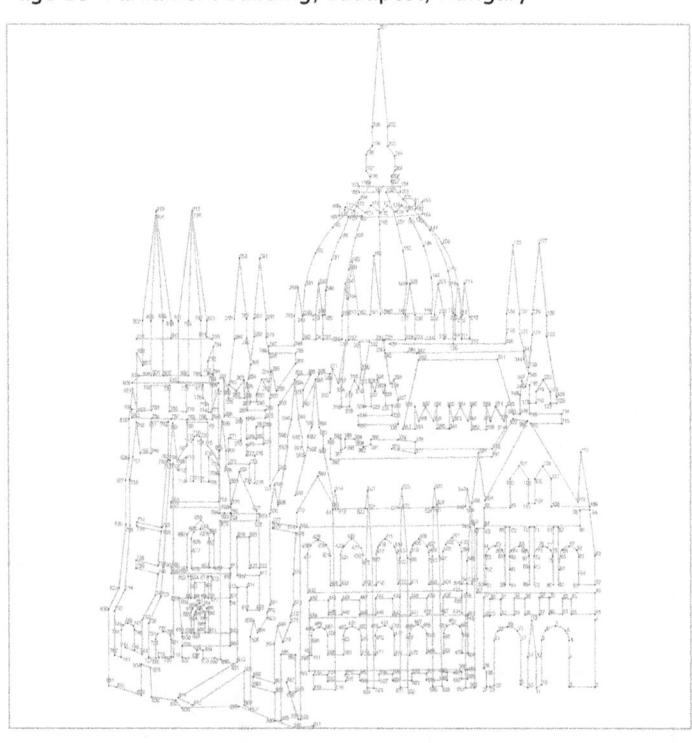

SOLUTIONS

Page 27: Milan Cathedral, Milan, Italy

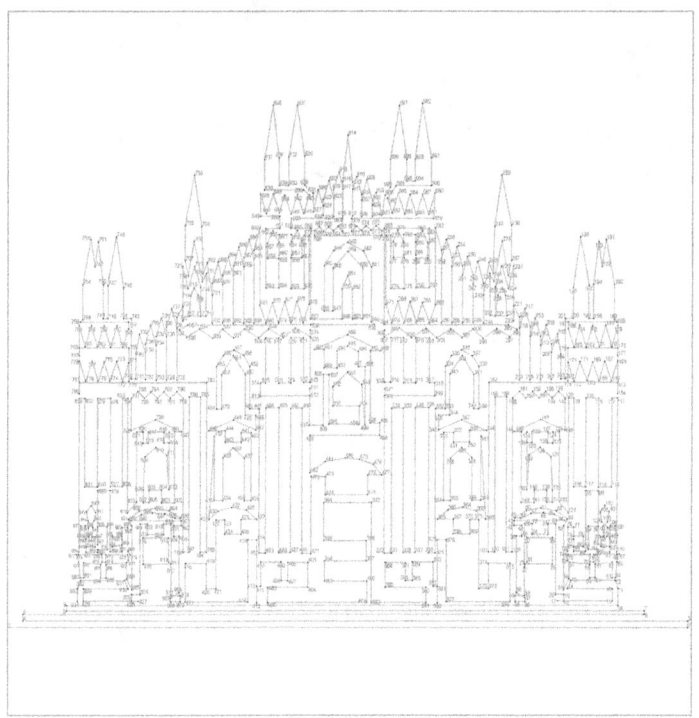

Page 29: Venice, Italy

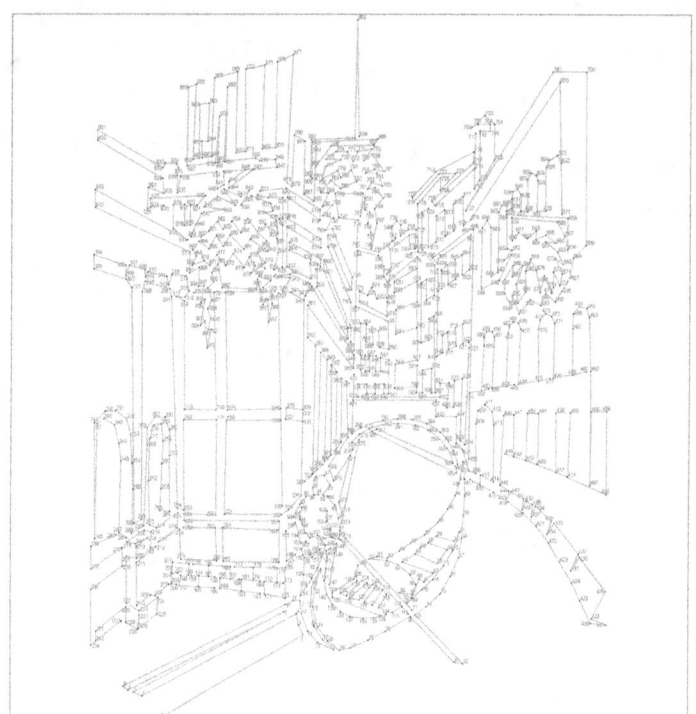

Page 31: Piazza del Campo, Siena, Italy

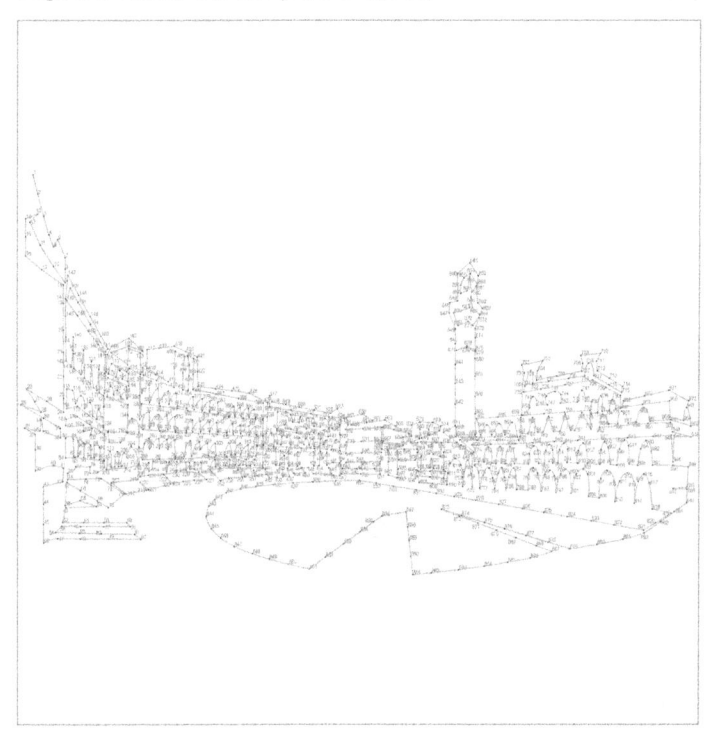

Page 33: Pantheon, Rome, Italy

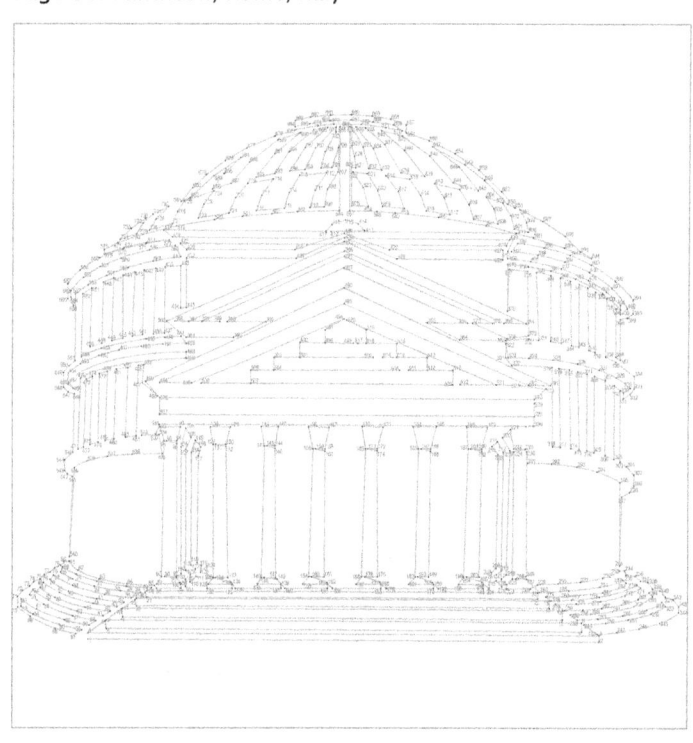

SOLUTIONS

Page 35: The Parthenon, Athens, Greece

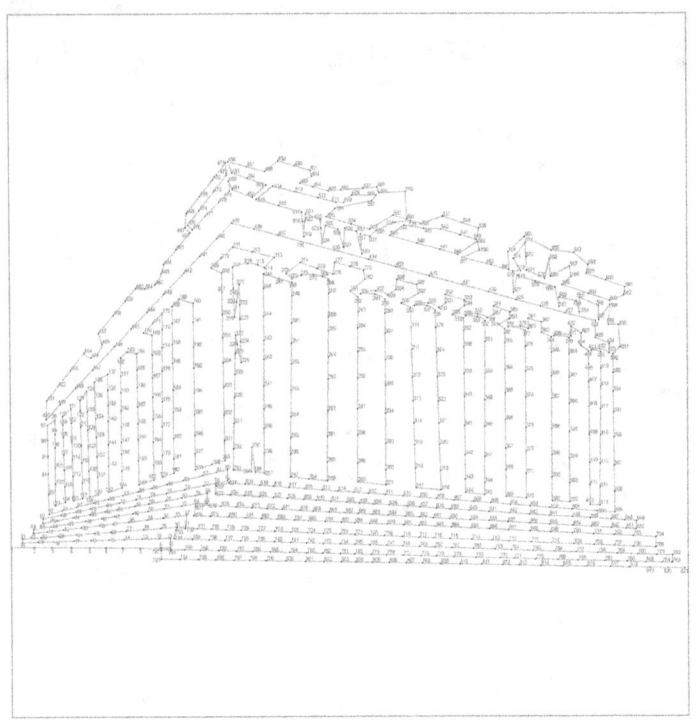

Page 37: Borgund Stave Church, Lardal, Norway

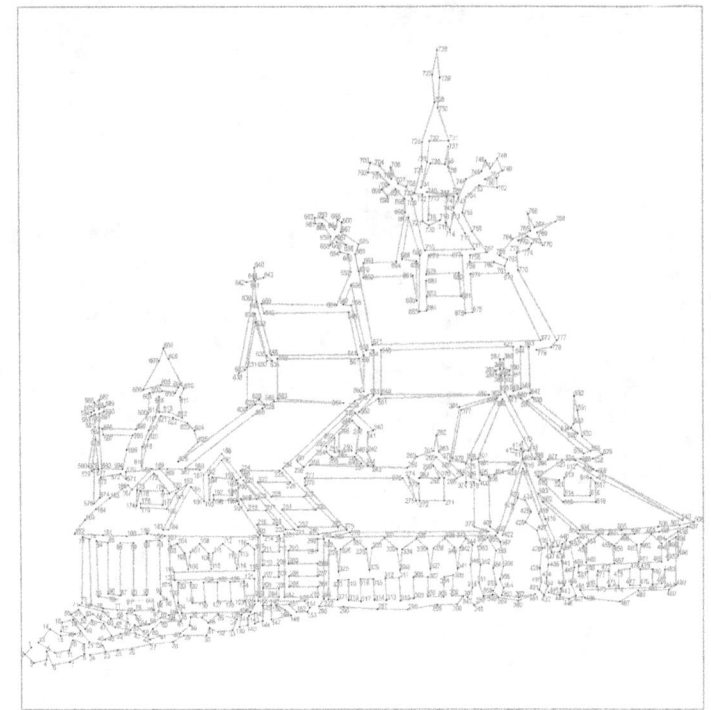

Page 39: Church of the Savior on Spilled Blood, St Petersburg, Russia

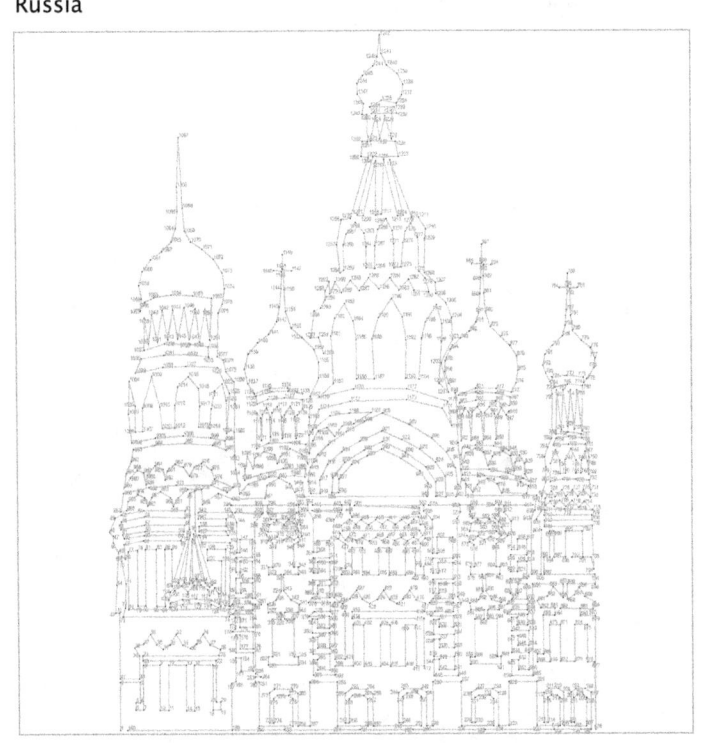

Page 41: Red Square, Moscow, Russia

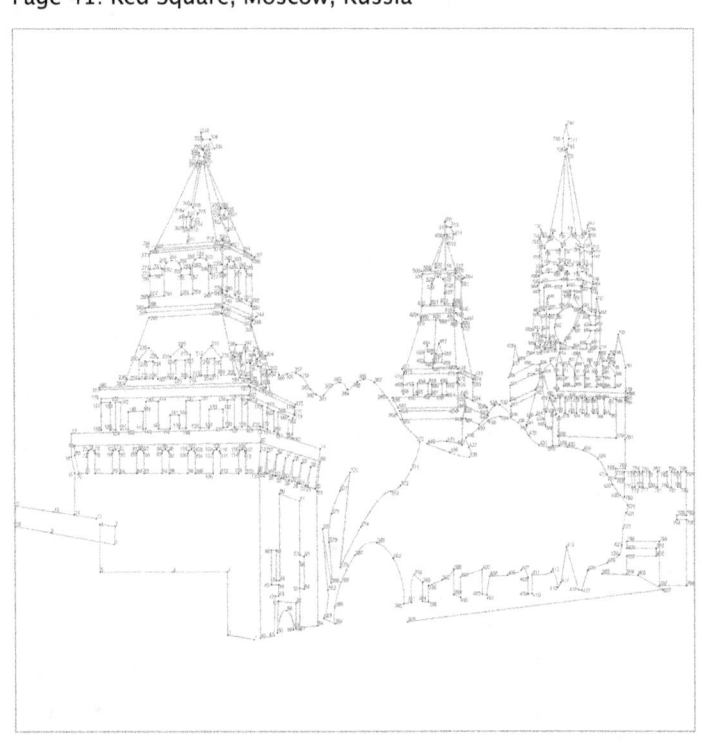

SOLUTIONS

Page 27: Milan Cathedral, Milan, Italy

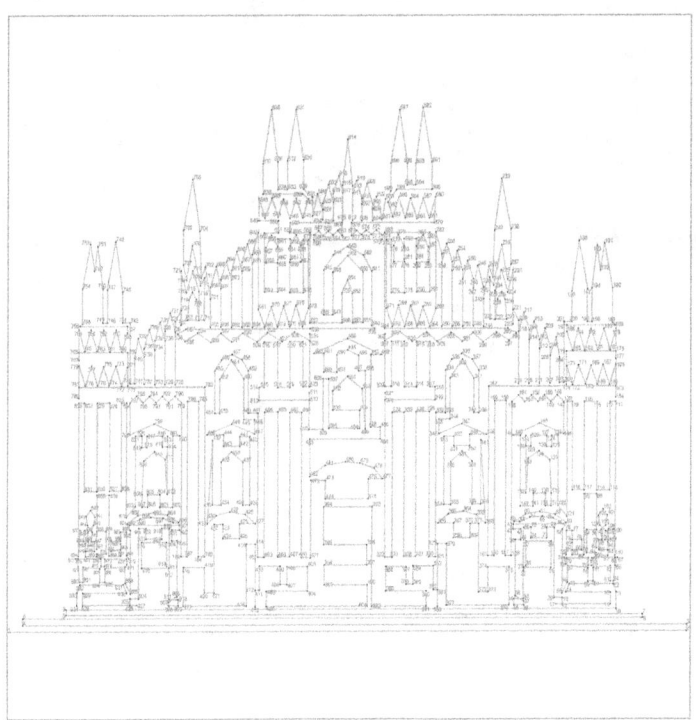

Page 29: Venice, Italy

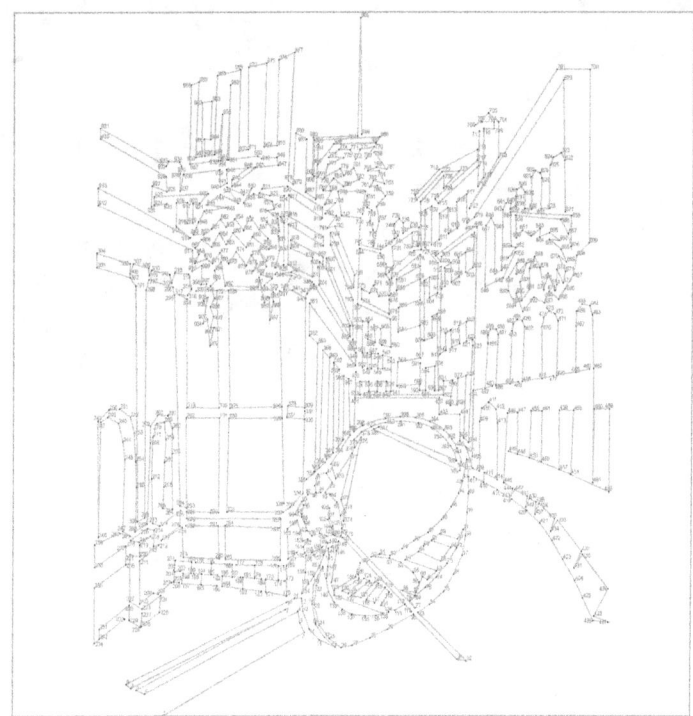

Page 31: Piazza del Campo, Siena, Italy

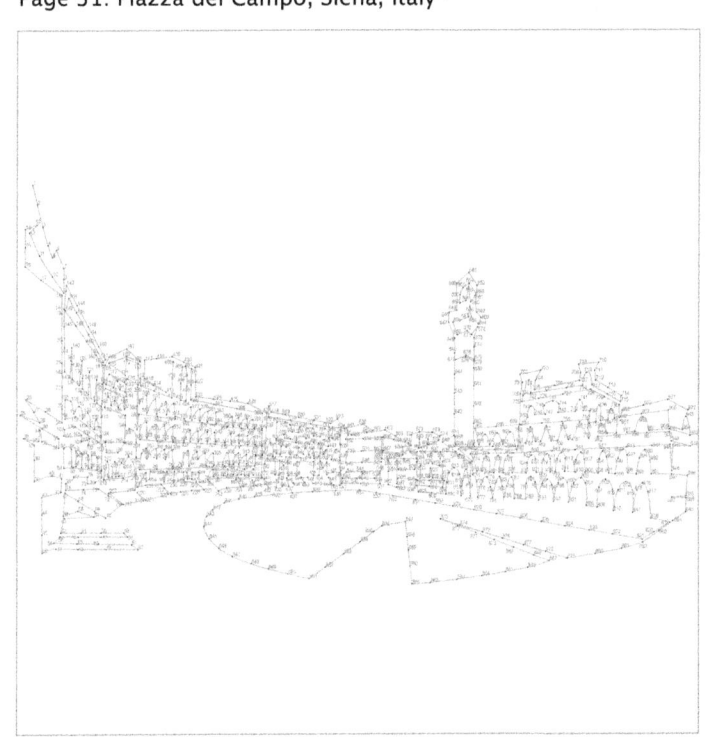

Page 33: Pantheon, Rome, Italy

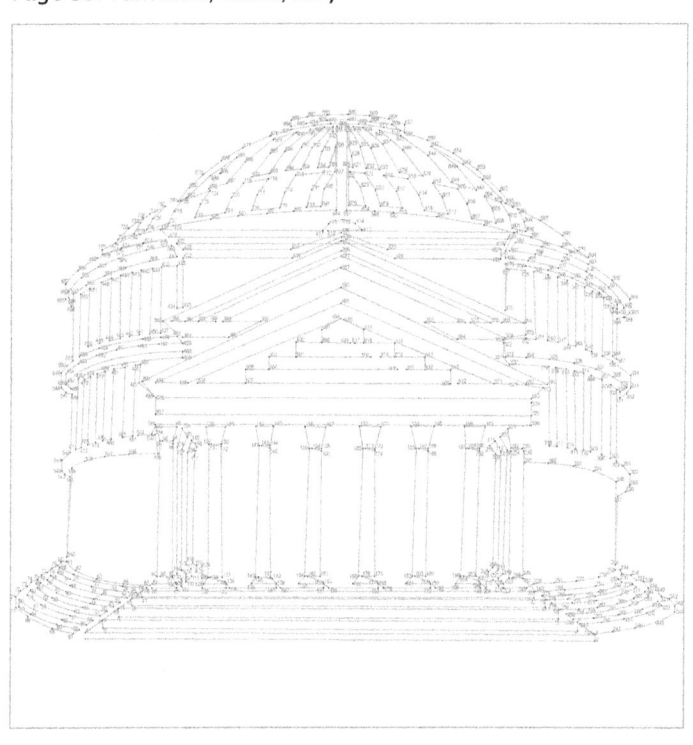

SOLUTIONS

Page 35: The Parthenon, Athens, Greece

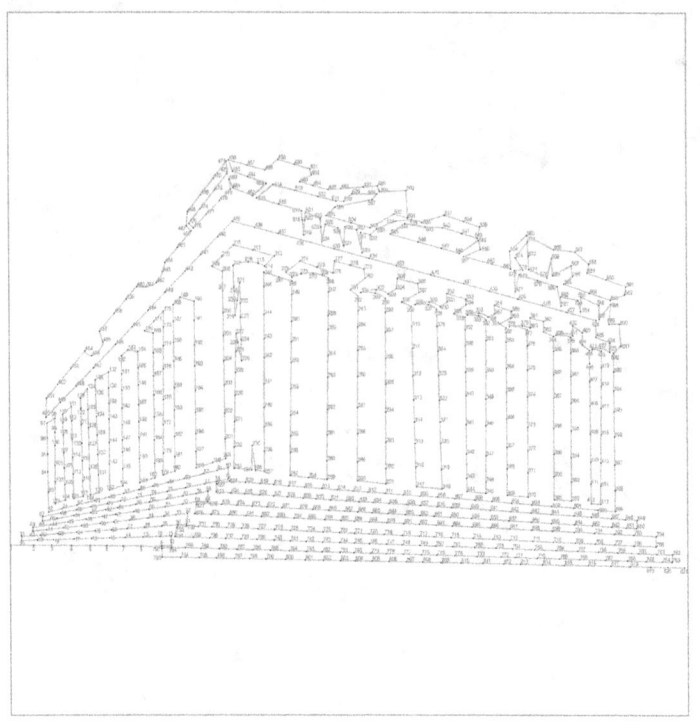

Page 37: Borgund Stave Church, Lardal, Norway

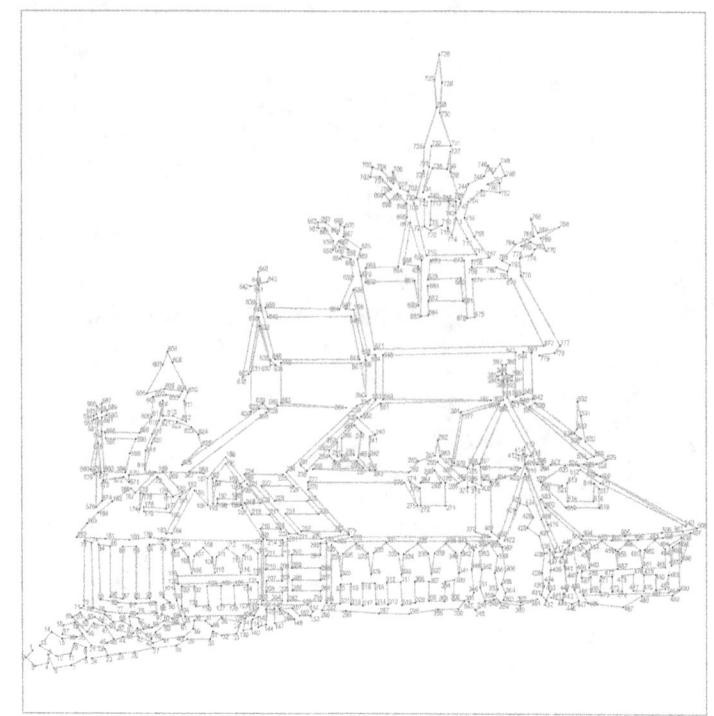

Page 39: Church of the Savior on Spilled Blood, St Petersburg, Russia

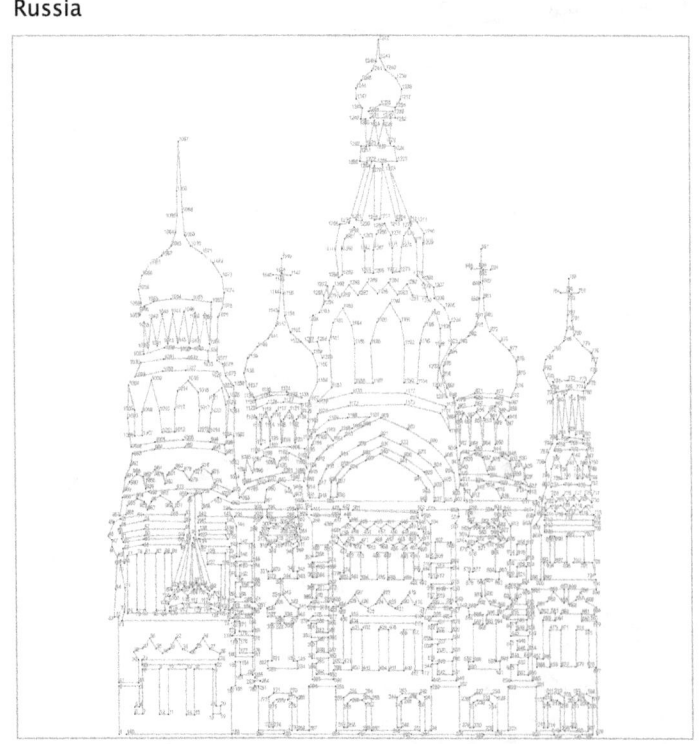

Page 41: Red Square, Moscow, Russia

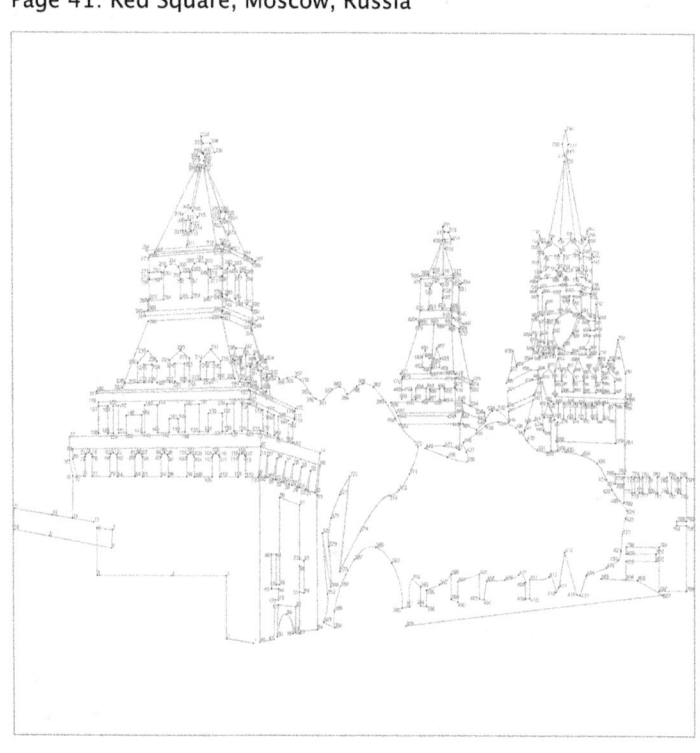

SOLUTIONS

Page 43: Hohensalzburg Fortress, Salzburg, Austria

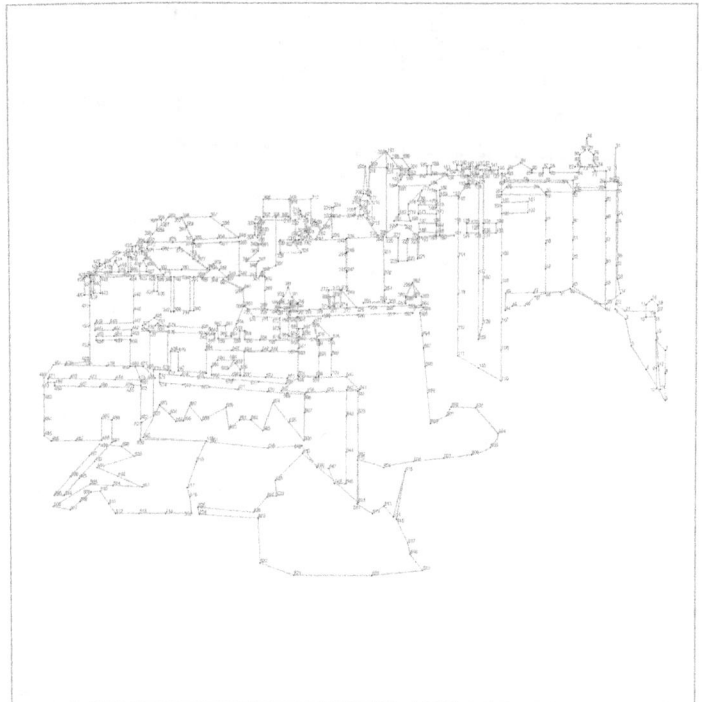

Page 45: The Burgtheater, Vienna, Austria

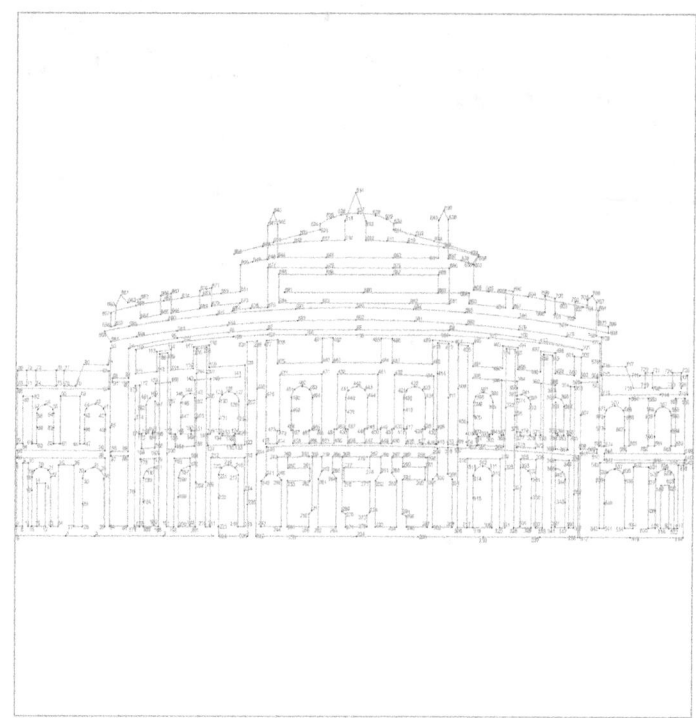

Page 47: Ha'penny Bridge, Dublin, Ireland

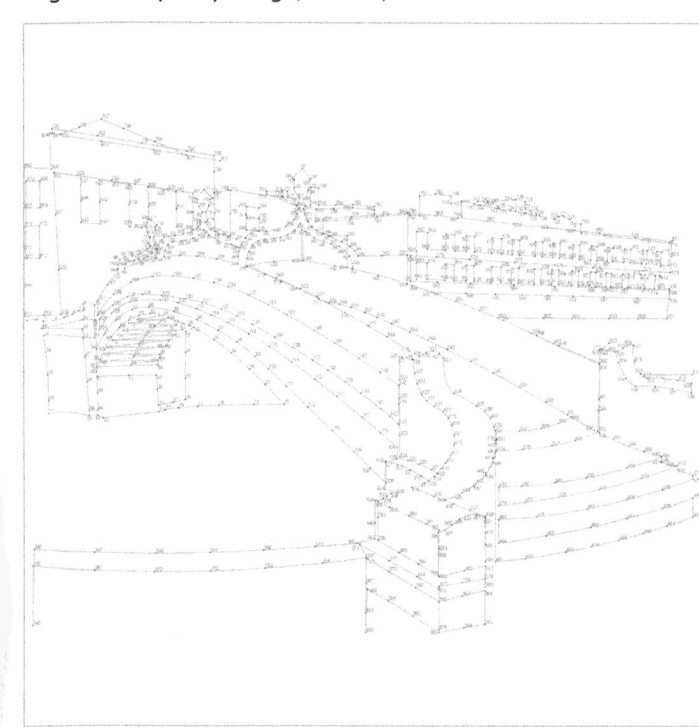